TULSA

B. Marie

Tulsa
B. Marie
Edited by <name>

Copyright © 2017 by B. Marie. All rights reserved.
No part of this book may be used or reproduced in
any manner whatsoever without the express written permission of the author.

For editorial inquiries, please contact B. Marie,
Bmbarros55@gmail.com.
First Edition

ISBN-13: 978-1548982140

Printed in the United States of America

Dedication

I dedicate this book to my family the descendants of Jack and Daisy Scott, Juanita, Julius, Eloise, Panchita, Sidney, Pauline, Guy, Altamese, Jonetta, Cris and Toussaint, along with all of the survivors of the Tulsa massacre. During this dark time in our nation's history survivors had to endure hatred, racism and overcome life's awful turn of events.

This book will hopefully educate not only the descendants but America as well, to what happened in history. Let the truth be told in all schools across America and in every classroom not just in Tulsa, Oklahoma but as part of American history.

To my children Stephanie, Angel, Shelby, Tre and my grandchildren Quinci and Christian may you continue to grow and learn the truth of your family and how strong, resilient and resourceful they had to be. Carry this message of hope with you throughout your lifetime.

I also dedicate this book to my friend and writing coach Jesse Sharpe. Thank you for the direction and encouragement to continue to tell this story.

I would be remiss if I did not include Kathy Dubrovsky, former librarian/coordinator of Sharon Public Schools for your encouragement to pursue this book to completion. Finally, Leslie Shapiro and Lisa Fireman thank you both for your many hours of editing, meetings and encouragement toward me. Without your input I don't think I would be able to have reached completion.

Much love to all of you!

B.Marie

Introduction

The early 1900s in Tulsa, Oklahoma was filled with racial tension. Life between Blacks, who were called Negroes at the time, and whites was like an underground electrical current. Most of that tension was fueled because in the early 20th century Black people in Tulsa were prospering. Many businesses were black-owned. As such, the black community was self-sufficient and didn't need support from the white residents or the federal government. Successful Black businesses included churches, banks, theaters, retail stores, barbershops, and many other establishments. Tulsa's Black residents also had their own Black school system, Black teachers and Black students from the Greenwood, Archer and Pine areas, and Negro teachers taught those students.

Oil was discovered in the early 1900s in the newly acquired state of Oklahoma. As a result, new wealth poured into the "Oil Capital of the World," particularly the Tulsa area. This provided many Blacks the opportunity to become so affluent, that Tulsa became known as the "Black Wall Street." My own grandparents, Jack and Daisy Scott, were landowners and business owners in Tulsa. My grandmother was a political cartoonist for the Tulsa Star Newspaper. My grandfather was a professional boxer.

Tulsa

By
B. Marie

TULSA

It was the first day of my summer vacation, June 1, 1921. This was going to be a great summer! I made the baseball team, and I was going to work with Daddy and make some money this summer. My birthday had just passed and now that I'm ten, Momma said it would be okay for me to ride my new bike across the railroad tracks downtown instead of just around the neighborhood.

I lazily got out of bed and walked out to the kitchen where Momma was cooking breakfast.
"Morning Julius", Momma said, looking over her shoulder at me when I came through the door. I yawned, stretched, and said, "Good morning."

"Time for you to start your first day down at the store. Eat your breakfast and go help your daddy."

"Okay," I said as I sat down at the kitchen table to eat the pancakes and bacon Momma had fixed for me,.

At that moment daddy came rushing through the door, "They did it! They finally did it! They're burning down the town. We've got to get outta here."

"What are you talking about, Jack?" Momma shouted.

"The white folks are burning down the town! Grab the kids and a few things we'll need. We've gotta get outta here, NOW!"

Momma stood there looking between me and Daddy. She was not sure what to do. She could not imagine just throwing all of their belongings in a few suitcases and leaving their home, their friends.

"Get going, Daisy," Daddy shouted.

Momma ran into the bedroom and started stuffing clothes into a large suitcase. Before running back into the kitchen, she picked up Baby Sister from her crib.

I helped out too. I grabbed a few toys for me and Baby Sister. When I looked out the kitchen window, all I could see was smoke billowing from downtown near Greenwood and Archer Streets. That was where Daddy had his grocery store; Junior's daddy, Mr. Lewis had his barbershop; and Mr. Terry's furniture store was also there. Thick black smoke rose from downtown where most of the other black owned businesses were.

Momma shouted as she ran back into the room, "What's going on Jack? What's happening?"

"Honey, whites folks have gone crazy. They're burning down the town. They've been angry for years now and it's finally come to a boil. They're enraged we're doing better than they are because we own most of this town. We have so many black owned businesses that are successful."

Momma crossed her arms. "That's nothing new, Jack. What really happened?"

"People are saying Dick Rowland touched a white woman in one of the elevators downtown and white men are trying to lynch him. A few former WWI black men went down to the jail to stop it. Things started to explode. Whites are setting things off shooting any Negroes they see. We gotta get outta here. They're burning down all the homes and buildings on our side of the tracks."

Daddy showed Momma his ripped shirt.
"I was barely able to get outta the store."

Daddy ran in and out of the house, grabbing whatever he could to load into the truck. He stopped just for a minute to answer Momma.

Daddy grabbed some food, blankets, his rifle, his pistol, and a bucket of bullets. He loaded us in the truck with whatever else he could carry, and we raced toward the opposite end of town.

White men from all over town could be seen gathering on the street corners where chaos ensued. As we raced away, I looked back and could see my whole town in flames. White men were running with torches, rifles and guns in hand. Smoke was everywhere!

As we rode, I saw Freddy Brown and his family loading up their car, Mazzie Parker and some other kids and their families, along with some of Momma and Daddy's friends scurrying to leave town as well. I looked back and could see my whole town in flames., smoke was everywhere!

Holding tightly to Daddy's arm as I rode beside him in the truck, I could see that the Five & Dime, the Baptist church, the big bank, and my school were all burning down.

Off in the distance I spotted airplanes flying towards Tulsa. I was shocked and scared when bombs started dropping from the planes. I began to shake uncontrollably and pleaded for Daddy to drive faster. He accelerated our truck as fast as it would go. As I glanced up at him, it was the first time in my life I saw fear in Daddy's eyes.
.

I looked back at my hometown with tears running down my face. How could people be so mean? Where we would go? How would we get through this? Daddy wrapped his arm around my shoulder and said, "Don't worry son. We will be okay."

Tulsa Before the Riot, During the Riot and After the Riot

The neighborhood where the rioting took place.

One of many black businesses in Tulsa during the 1920s.

Grocery store in Tulsa during the 1920s.

Negro children taught by Negro teachers in their black owned schools.

Life during the early 20th century!

Downtown Tulsa after the bombings!

Children with nowhere to go after the bombing of their city Tulsa.

Families loaded up trying to escape the rioting and bombing of Tulsa, Oklahoma.

Camps where many residents fled outside of Tulsa once they had nowhere to go.

A woman sitting in one of the camps after the bombing.

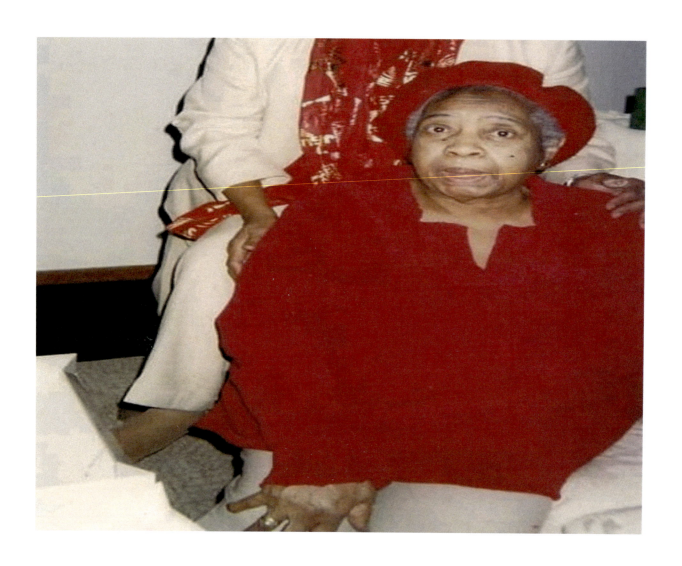

My aunt Juanita Parry, Survivor of the Tulsa Massacre, and daughter of Jack and Daisy Scott.

My Uncle Julius Scott, a Tulsa Massacre Survivor, son of Jack and Daisy Scott.

My grandmother Daisy Scott political cartoonist for the Tulsa Star newspaper and Massacre survivor.

Jack and Daisy Scott survivors of the Tulsa Massacre! My grandparents.

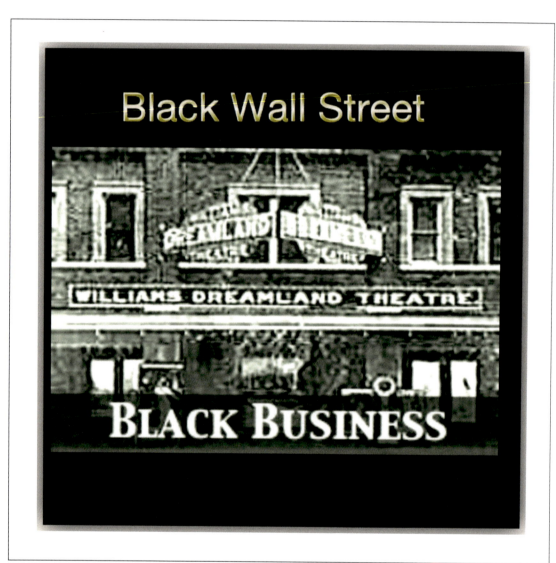

Tulsa Massacre Survivors front row.

BOXERS READY TO GO

Middleweights for Friday's Show Completo Training.

Jack Scott and George Clark, the two middleweights who furnish the main event of 10 rounds in tomorrow night's D. M. A C. smoker, will finish their training at the club this afternoon and will be ready for the contest which many fans enthusiasticly declare will be the fastest middleweight contest staged in Tulsa since the Jimmie McDonald-Jimmie Kelly contest at the Grand five years ago. Some exceptional preliminary talent has been engaged in which Tobe Roach and Knockout Brown figure in the semi-final.

Newspaper clipping of Jack Scott's boxing match.

In the days, weeks and months that followed the Tulsa riots, and bombings by the US Marshalls, hundreds of black residents had their homes and business looted, set afire, and many hundreds were killed by angry white mobs. Those that survived were housed in Red Cross camps outside of the city. Many families eventually moved away from Tulsa, while others stayed and tried to rebuild their lives.

To this day the black survivors of this devastating period in US history have not been compensated for the loss they endured, while white survivors were compensated immediately. Even after enlisting the services of famous attorney, Johnny Cochran, no Black families received reparations by the federal government. Even though Tulsa has rebuilt, it has never regained its status of Black Wall St.

As of the writing of this book, my own uncle Julius Scott, a Tulsa survivor, recently passed away on January 13, 2018 at the tender age of 96 in Tulsa, Oklahoma. His sister, Juanita Parry, also a survivor passed away in June 2007. They were never compensated for what they and their parents, Jack and Daisy Scott, lost during this shameful and appalling period in our nation's history.

Made in the USA
Middletown, DE
10 March 2022